Snook
in a
Book

I0167538

Written by Christie Motz
Illustrated by QBN Studios

I dedicate this book with love to the two most important Ted's in my life: My father Ted, who inspired this book, and my son Teddy, who inspires me every day.

Long, long ago
In a land far away,
Stood the City of Snook
Where all the snooks play.

"What's a snook," you ask?
Well, they're like you and like me.
Except a snook LOVES books
They're reading constantly.

The City of Snook
Has a wonderful leader
He's the snook of all snooks.
A snook Super Reader!

Build Creativity
Imagine New Worlds
Learn New Things

He discovered that reading,
Is the most magical thing.
If you can read,
You can do ANYTHING!

Whatever you wish
To grow up and do
Fight dragons, build bridges
or visit the moon

Simply can't be done
Without one magical deed
To make your dreams come true
You MUST learn to READ!

The Super Reader decided
The perfect job for the snooks
Was to help children discover
The magic of books!

He then gave each snook
An important mission.
And sent them to Earth,
Under his supervision.

Happy and excited
And a bit nervous too
Each snook accepted their mission,
And found their way to you!

It's your lucky day
If a snook visits you.
When you find a snook at your door,
Here is what you must do:

Hug it and love it
Put it in a special place.
Then read books to it!
That will put a smile on its face.

At night, it will travel back,
To the City of Snook
And report to the Super Reader
What you've been doing with books!

In the morning, it will return
Without ever being caught
So when you see it, hurry quick!
And start reading on the spot.

A snook loves nothing more
Than listening to you.
Reading is magical!
And you've got the magic in YOU.

So, gather your favorite stories
And find a cozy nook.
Discover the magic of reading,
With a Snook in a Book!

ABOUT THE AUTHOR

Christie Motz is a former kindergarten teacher and mother of three. During her nine years in the classroom, her biggest delight was inspiring a lifelong *love* of reading in her students through inventive methods. *Snook in a Book* is based on her amazing real life experiences as a teacher. She is passionate about empowering young readers and bringing joy to their lives through the magic of reading books. *Snook in a Book* is her first publication.

ILLUSTRATOR BIO

QBN Studios is a small Illustration studio located in Vernon, Connecticut. Owners Quynh Nguyen and Christopher MacCoy are passionate about helping authors fulfill their dreams and bring their words to life. QBN Studio's goal is to create an immersive experience for their audiences, to tumble headfirst into imaginary worlds. Follow us on Instagram @qbnstudios for the latest updates on illustrations, books, and other projects.

www.qbnstudios.com

www.ingramcontent.com/pod-product-compliance
Lightning Source LLC
LaVergne TN
LVHW072135070426
835513LV00003B/108